A New True Book

EXPERIMENTS WITH WATER

By Ray Broekel

CHILDRENS PRESS ®

CHICAGO

Water magnifies objects.

PHOTO CREDITS

Journalism Services:
© John Bowen—4, 42
© Dirk Gallian—39 (left), 45
© Joseph Jacobson—Cover, 2, 7 (2 photos), 8,
10, 14, 15 (2 photos), 16 (right), 18 (2 photos),
19, 20 (2 photos), 21 (2 photos), 22 (3 photos),
23 (bottom), 24 (2 photos), 25, 26 (2 photos),
27, 28, 30 (2 photos), 32 (2 photos), 34, 36, 38
(2 photos), 39 (right), 40 (2 photos), 41
© John Patsch—16 (left)

Tom Stack and Associates:
© Jeff March—23 (top)

Art: John Forsberg—5
    Tom Dunnington—13

Cover: Refraction of light causes the split
images in the glass.

*for **Matthew***

Library of Congress Cataloging-in-Publication Data

Broekel, Ray.
  Experiments with water.

  (A New true book)
  Includes index.
  Summary: Presents experiments which demonstrate
the properties of water.
  1. Water—Experiments—Juvenile literature.
[1. Water—
Experiments. 2. Experiments] I. Title.
QC920.B76   1988   546'.22   87-34147
ISBN 0-516-01215-0

Childrens Press®, Chicago
Copyright ©1988 by Regensteiner Publishing Enterprises, Inc.
All rights reserved. Published simultaneously in Canada.
Printed in the United States of America.
    3 4 5 6 7 8 9 10 R 97 96 95 94 93 92 91 90

TABLE OF CONTENTS

WHAT IS WATER?

Water is found everywhere on earth. It covers over 75 percent of the earth's surface.

All living things need water. Water makes up about two-thirds of the human body. Blood and other fluids in our bodies are composed mostly of water.

5

Water is made of two basic parts called elements. An element is a substance that cannot be broken down into different substances. The two elements in water are the gases hydrogen and oxygen. When these two gases are together in the proper amount—two atoms of hydrogen to every atom of oxygen—they make water. The chemical name, or formula, for water is H_2O.

Water can be a liquid (far left) or a solid (left).

THE THREE FORMS OF WATER

Water is found in three forms. The first is the liquid form—water.

The second is the solid form—ice. When the water temperature drops below the freezing point, it forms ice.

Water leaves wet clothes in the form of vapor.

The third form of water is the invisible gas—vapor. If you boil water, it goes into the air as vapor. When you dry clothes outdoors, the water that leaves the wet clothes goes into the air in the form of vapor.

WATER CAN CHANGE FORMS

Water can change forms in six ways.

Condensation is the change of water vapor into liquid water. Dew on the grass in the morning comes from water vapor.

Evaporation takes place when liquid water changes to water vapor. The sun changes the dew back into water vapor.

When water vapor freezes it falls to the ground as snow.

Freezing is the changing of liquid water to ice.

Melting is the changing of ice to liquid water.

Sublimation is the name given to two kinds of

changes. The first kind of
sublimation happens when
ice or snow changes to water
vapor, usually when the
sun shines on it. The ice or
snow seems to disappear
without melting first.

Another kind of
sublimation takes place
when the air temperature
drops below freezing and
water vapor quickly
changes to ice without
becoming a liquid first.
The water vapor falls to
the ground as snow.

THE WATER CYCLE

Water is constantly changing from the liquid state to the vapor state and back again.

Evaporation takes place all the time. Most evaporation takes place from the surfaces of large bodies of water such as the oceans. But it can take place from anything that contains water.

When water vapor changes back to liquid

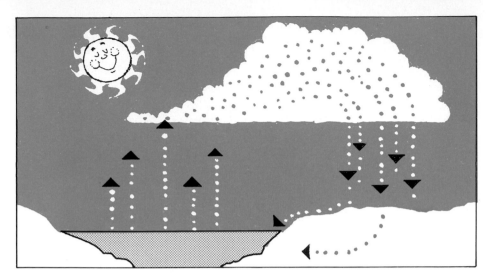

Water evaporates into the air as vapor. It returns to the earth as either rain or snow. This process is called the water cycle.

water, it is said to condense. Water that evaporates into the air eventually condenses again. The condensation then falls as either rain or snow, depending on the temperature. This process is called the water cycle.

These experiments will help you to understand the water cycle.

EXPERIMENTS

Equipment:
stove or hot plate
water
pot
ruler
glass

1. Ask an adult to help you with this experiment. Heat a pot of water until the water begins to boil. Now with an adult watching, carefully put the glass on the end of the ruler and hold it over the pot. What happens? Where did the drops of water come from?

   Water is made up of tiny, invisible molecules. When heated, molecules at the surface of water will escape into the air as water vapor.

Water vapor will condense on the mirror.

When water vapor cools and condenses upon something, it changes into water again. That is why moisture has formed on the glass.

2. You can experiment with water vapor using your own body. When you take in air you inhale. When you breathe out you exhale. And whether you inhale or exhale, some water is transferred.

You take in much more water than your body needs. Some of this is returned to the air as water vapor when you exhale. You cannot see it because it leaves your mouth as a gas. But you can see it if it condenses. Try breathing on a mirror. What happens? The mirror

In cold weather you can see water vapor (left). The girl
at right shows how moving air speeds evaporation.

becomes cloudy, this shows the
presence of water vapor.

You can see water vapor on a cold
winter day. When you exhale, the water
vapor you exhaled is condensed in the
cold air and it is visible.

3. Evaporation takes place faster when
air is in motion. See if that is true. Draw
two squares on a chalkboard. Make certain
the squares are at least three feet apart.
Squeeze a sponge above them to cover the
squares with water.

Now fan one of the squares. Which
square dries faster?

When you fan the air, you put air in
motion. Air in motion picks up more
moisture. You have proved it.

WATER
DISSOLVES THINGS

Water dissolves things. It dissolves some things more easily than it does others. Cocoa, salt, and sugar dissolve easily in water. These things can also be dissolved in other liquids such as oil or milk. But water is the best solvent for them.

Try the following experiments.

EXPERIMENTS

1. Fill a glass with water. Then dissolve salt in it. How long does it take before the salt is completely dissolved? Now try dissolving salt in milk or oil. How long does this take? Try this same experiment with hot water, milk, and oil. How long did it take for the salt to dissolve?

   The hotter the liquid, the quicker the rate of dissolving. The colder the liquid, the longer it takes. Water is a good solvent for many things.

   Try these experiments using cocoa or sugar.

Girl experiments with sugar.

Do small solids dissolve faster than large ones?

Equipment:
2 sugar cubes   paper
hammer   2 glasses

2. Items that are broken into small pieces generally will dissolve more quickly than will whole items.

Put one cube on the paper and hit it with the hammer so that it breaks into fine pieces.

Now fill the two glasses with equal amounts of water. At the same time, drop the whole sugar cube into one glass, and pour the broken cube into the other glass. What do you observe? In which glass is the sugar dissolving more quickly?

After a day the solids in the water (left)
will settle to the bottom (right).

3. When water can't dissolve things, they
separate from the water.
    You will need a jar of muddy water
from a roadside puddle. Stir the water in
the jar and then allow it to sit for a day.
Examine the jar the next day.
    What do you find? The water is now
clear. The bits of dirt that were
suspended in the water have now
settled. Soil does not dissolve in water,
so it eventually settles to the bottom.

WATER EXPANDS WHEN IT FREEZES

The ice cube tray and the milk container show what happens when water freezes.

When water freezes it takes up more space. It expands. You can prove this yourself.

EXPERIMENTS

1. Fill a plastic milk container with water. Press the cap down firmly. Now freeze the container.

   As the water inside the container freezes, it will expand. What do you see? Has the cap pushed up? Are there any bulges?

This experiment shows how water expands and contracts at different temperatures.

2. Water is not like any other liquid. It starts to expand even before it reaches the freezing point 32°F. (0°C.). At about 39°F. (4°C) water starts to expand. Then it contracts as the temperature drops.

You can prove this expansion by the following experiment. Fill a small bottle with colored water. Stop it with a cork that has a thin glass tube through it. Press in the cork until the water rises a few inches in the tube. Mark the height on the paper you have attached to the tube.

Now bury the bottle in a glass of equal parts of cracked ice and salt. As the water cools, it goes down in the tube. Then further cooling causes it to rise again.

WATER HAS SURFACE TENSION

Surface tension can support the weight of this water strider.

Water and other liquids have a thin film that covers their surfaces. This film is called surface tension. You can experiment with surface tension.

Gently lower the needle into the water.

Equipment:
needle   fork   glass   water

1. Place the needle across the tines of the fork. Gently break the surface of the water with the tines. If you are careful, the needle will float as you take the fork away.

The needle (above) seems to bend the surface of the water. What happens when you carefully drop a penny into a full glass of water?

Look carefully at the water surface. Note how the surface film seems to bend under the weight of the needle.

Equipment:
glass   dry cloth   10 pennies

2. Rub the top edge of the glass with the dry cloth. Now pour water into the glass until it is full or even slightly above the top.

Now carefully drop a penny edgewise into the glass. Slowly drop in more pennies to see how high the water will go before running over the side. Surface tension holds the water above the rim of the glass.

What happens to
the talcum powder
when the soap
touches the water?

Equipment:
large plate
talcum powder
piece of soap

3. Fill a clean plate with cold water. Put
    it on a table and let it stand until the
    water surface is quiet.
    Now sprinkle talcum powder lightly
    over the surface of the water. Wet a
    piece of soap and touch the soap to the
    water near the edge of the plate.
    The talcum powder will be drawn to
    the opposite side of the plate at once.
    What has happened? The soap has
    reduced the surface tension at one point
    and increased it on the other sides. The
    increased tension pulls the talcum
    powder with it.

How can five streams of water be made to flow into a single stream?

Equipment: tin can water

4. Ask an adult to make five holes near the bottom of the can about one-quarter inch apart.

Now put the can over a sink and fill it with water. Notice that the water comes out in streams from each of the holes.

Now use your thumb and forefinger to pinch the jets of water together. You have now made one stream from five. Surface tension holds them together.

To again make the stream into five separate ones, just brush your hand across the holes. The streams will

separate.

You can explore surface tension in different liquids.

Equipment:
glass   eyedropper
water   vegetable oil

What happens when you drop oil into a glass of water?

5. Squirt a few drops of oil under the surface of the water. Some will stop under the surface. Some will rise above the surface and flatten out.

The surface tension of the water holds some of the drops of oil below the water's surface. The surface tension of the oil pulls these drops into the form of a sphere.

When a drop of oil breaks the water's surface, the oil surface tension cannot support the weight of the oil as a sphere, so it flattens out.

WATER HAS ADHESION

When water molecules cling to glass it is called adhesion. For example, adhesion can cause water to climb up the sides of a jar. Try this experiment.

EXPERIMENT

Get the thinnest glass bottle or vase you can find. Now fill the bottle halfway with water. Compare the sides of the water with the middle part. Are the sides higher? This is adhesion. The thinner the glass, the more clearly you can see the adhesion.

THE CAPILLARY ACTION OF WATER

Capillary action takes place when water climbs uphill. The water molecules climb upward when in contact with an absorbent material such as a sponge or blotter. Try the following experiment.

EXPERIMENT

1. Fill a shallow dish with water. Now dip a sponge or a blotter into the water. What happens? The water moves up into the blotter or sponge. This is capillary action.

29

This experiment shows how water climbs uphill.

Equipment:

2 small, flat pieces of glass   transparent tape
water
soap   food coloring

2. You can make water rise between two pieces of glass.

First, clean the two pieces of glass with soap and water. Now place two thicknesses of transparent tape on the inside corners of one piece of glass. Now hold the two pieces together and dip the bottom edge into a pan of colored water. What happens?

Now try to pull the panes of glass apart. You will find that hard to do unless you slide them apart.

WATER AND HEAT

Water warms up and cools down more slowly than does soil. This is why summers are cooler and the winters are milder near the ocean than they are inland. You can demonstrate this yourself.

Equipment:
2 shallow pans (same size)
2 thermometers

EXPERIMENT

Fill one pan with water, the other with soil. Place one thermometer in each pan. Make certain both thermometers show

How does water temperature differ from soil temperature?
Which one heats up and cools down faster?

the same temperature. You can adjust the temperature of the water by adding more hot or cold water.

Now leave both pans in a sunny place for about twenty minutes. Read the temperature again. What has happened?

Now allow the temperature to come down to the same level in both pans. Then place both pans in a refrigerator for about twenty minutes. Remove the pans and read the temperatures again. What has now happened? What have you proved by the two experiments?

WATER AND LIGHT

When you look into water, your eyes are often fooled. Why? The answer is that light rays have been bent when they entered the water.

You can see bending of light rays in water by doing this simple experiment.

The pencil in the glass is an example of the refraction of light.

EXPERIMENT

Put a pencil into a glass of water. Look down into the glass. Does the pencil appear to be broken?

The reason for this is that the light rays have been bent as they passed from air into water. This is called refraction of light. Water is much more dense than air, so light rays travel more slowly in water. This causes refraction. And you see what seems to be a broken pencil.

WATER MAGNIFIES

Water in a curved container magnifies. In the last experiment, the part of the pencil in the water appeared to be larger than the part in the air. This is because of the shape of the jar. There is more water at the center of a round jar than at the sides. Light rays coming into the jar are therefore

bent, or refracted. The
water acts as a magnifying
glass, and the object looks
larger than its real size.
Try this experiment.

Water magnifies.

EXPERIMENT:

Equipment:
round jar
water
2 coins

Fill the jar with water. Place one coin in
the jar and one next to the jar. Which
coin appears to be larger? Why? Try the
experiment with pairs of other small
objects.

WATER HAS PRESSURE

Water has weight and pressure. Water weighs about 8-1/3 pounds per gallon. So it has pressure if it sits on top of something.

The more water there is on the top of something, the greater will be the pressure at the bottom. You can demonstrate this.

Which hole shoots out the farthest steam of water?

EXPERIMENT

Equipment:
  tall tin can   hammer
  heavy nail   adhesive tape

Ask an adult to punch holes up the side of the can. Place the holes about 1/8 inch apart, starting from the bottom. Now cover the holes with a strip of adhesive tape.

Hold the can over a sink and fill it to the top with water. Quickly pull off the tape, starting at the bottom. What happens? Which holes shoot out streams of water the farthest? What does this show?

THE BUOYANCY OF WATER

Buoyancy means to have the ability to float in water. The shape of things and the amount of air inside them determine their buoyancy. Test this yourself.

What is the difference between an empty can and a full can in this experiment?

EXPERIMENT

Equipment:
coffee can   water
  with plastic top   bucket

1. Fill the bucket with water. With the cover on the bottom, push the empty can completely into the bucket. What happens?
    This time push the can halfway into the bucket of water. What happens now?
    Fill the can half full of water and put the lid back on. Repeat the two experiments above. What happens to the can?
    Now completely fill the can with water. Try the experiments again. What happens to the can?

Why does one object float and the other sink?

Equipment:
2 pieces of aluminum foil
water
bucket

2. Fill the bucket with water. Shape one
    piece of foil into a little boat. Float the
    boat on the water.
       Wad the other piece of foil into a ball
    and try to float it on the water. What
    happens? Why does the aluminum boat
    float while the aluminum ball sinks?

41

THINGS TO REMEMBER

Water is everywhere. It covers more than 75 percent of the earth. All living things need water. Water is found in three forms: liquid, the solid form called ice, and the gaseous form called water vapor.

Evaporation is the change from liquid form to water vapor. Evaporation takes place all the time. When the water vapor condenses, it becomes a liquid again. This process is called the water cycle.

Water dissolves things. Water is the best solvent in which things can be dissolved.

Water expands when it freezes. Ice floats on the surface of water because it is less dense than liquid water.

Water and other liquids have a thin film that covers their surfaces. This surface film is called surface tension.

Water warms up and cools off more slowly than does the land around it.

Water has weight and pressure. Water weighs about 8-1/3 pounds per gallon. So water exerts pressure on things.

Buoyancy means having the ability to float in water. Some things are more buoyant than others.

WORDS YOU SHOULD KNOW

adhesion(ad•HEE•jun)—the cling of water molecules to glass

buoyancy(BOY•en•cee)—the ability to float in water

capillary action(KAP•ih•lair•ee ACK•shun)—the movement of water when it climbs uphill

condensation(kahn•den•SAY•shun)—the change of water vapor to a liquid

dissolve(dih•ZOLV)—to become part of water or some other liquid

element(EL•ih•ment)—a substance that cannot be broken down into different substances

evaporation(ih•vap•er•RAY•shun)—the change of water to water vapor

exhale(ex•HAIL)—to breathe out air and water vapor

H₂O—the chemical name for water

ice(EISS)—the solid form of water

inhale(in•HAIL)—to breathe in air and water vapor

pressure(PRESH•er)—the force of one thing pushing against another

refraction(re•FRACK•shun)—the bending of light rays passing into water

solvent(SAHL•vent)—a liquid that causes other substances to dissolve

sublimation(sub•blih•MAY•shun)—when a solid changes to a gas, or the other way around

surface tension(SER•fiss TEN•shun)—the thin film that covers the surface of a liquid

water vapor(WAW•ter VAY•per)—the gaseous state of water

water weight(WAW•ter WAIT)—a gallon of water weighs about 8-1/3 pounds

INDEX

ABOUT THE AUTHOR

Ray Broekel has been writing children's books for more than thirty years. He has written almost a book a year for Childrens Press. Dr. Broekel is well known in the publishing field as a teacher, editor, and author of science materials for young people.

A full-time freelance writer, Dr. Broekel has written many other kinds of books for both children and adults. He now has almost 200 published books to his credit. He is considered to be the number one authority on candy bar and chocolate history in the United States, having written several books and many articles on those subjects. He and his wife Peg live with their dog, Fergus, in Ipswich, Massachusetts.